TAO TE CHING DECODED

BOOKS BY KEVIN M THOMAS:

Commands of the New Testament
Why Daughters Need Their Dads
The Happiest Women
Chinese Spiritual Thoughts
The Great Path
Wisdom and Virtue
Tao Te Ching Decoded

TAO TE CHING DECODED

Book of Wisdom Path of Virtue

KEVIN M. THOMAS

© Copyright 2007, 2024 Kevin M. Thomas. All Rights Reserved

All rights reserved. No part of this book may be reproduced or transmitted in any form or by any means, electronic or mechanical, including photocopying, recording, or by any storage or retrieval system without permission in writing from copyright author.

For more information, address to KETNA Publishing
P.O. Box 90861, Burton, Michigan, 48509

First KETNA Printing Edition 2022

Cover Design By: Windlaugh
Book Interior and E-book Design by Amit Dey (amitdey2528@gmail.com)

is a registered trademark of KETNA Publishing

Printed in the USA

2007 Library of Congress Control Number: 2007900729
2024 Library of Congress Control Number: 2024918358

ISBN: 978-1-948265-11-9 (soft cover)
ISBN 978-1-948265-12-6 (hard cover)
ISBN 978-1-948265-13-3 (e-book)

DEDICATION

I wish to dedicate this book to my loving children, Isiah, Caroline, Kimberly, and Cheyenne. Their undying, patient, enthusiastic, and unconditional love motivates me to keep going. May they always understand my unconditional love I have for them.

I also write this book in honor of my supportive parents, June and Grover, who were there when I needed them the most, and now rest in the arm of Jesus.

ACKNOWLEDGMENTS

To my parents, June and Grover, I thank you for everything you did for me. I wish I could have done more to please you in this life. Thank you for trying to make me a better person and man. Could you put in a good word for me in Heaven?

Though miles separate us, my children Isiah, Caroline, Kimberly, and Cheyenne know that in my heart, I have unconditional love for you. Hopefully, someday, you will understand the real truth.

To those who have genuinely supported me, thank you. You know who you are.

TABLE OF CONTENTS

Dedication vii
Acknowledgments ix
Introduction xvii
  1. Follow the Right Path 1
  2. Live Without Judgment and Desire 2
  3. Be Humble and Treat People Well 3
  4. The Path Brings Love and Compassion 4
  5. You Must Live and Experience the Truth Path 5
  6. Mother Earth Flows 6
  7. The Path Never Ends 7
  8. Gently Present the Path to Others 8
  9. Don't Brag, Boast, or Demand Your Way 9
10. Let Go of Material Possessions and Give 10
11. Don't Clutter Your Brain with Useless Things 11
12. Avoid Distractions and Seek the Eternal 12

13. Be a Humble Servant 13
14. The Spirit is the Beginning of the Path 14
15. Make the Teachings of the Path Clear to All. 15
16. Plant a Seed in Others. 16
17. Make Your Path a Team Effort. 17
18. Be Wary of False Teachings 18
19. Avoid False Devotion to God 19
20. Following the Path Requires Sacrifice 20
21. The Path is Driven by Faith and Belief 21
22. The Path Has All the Answers 22
23. Only One Path is Complete 23
24. Don't Stray from the True Path 24
25. Four Things Are Great 25
26. Bear Your Heavy Burdens 26
27. Teach the Path without Criticism 27
28. Be an Example for Others. 28
29. Don't Try to Rule the World. 29
30. Avoid War and the Wrong Path 30
31. Avoid Using Weapons Whenever Possible 31
32. You Don't Need a Fancy Title to Follow the Path 32

33. True Power is Understanding Yourself and Others. . . . 33
34. The Path Reveals its Greatness if You Stay on It 34
35. The Path Will Bring You Rest and Peace. 35
36. Empty the Old You and Begin the New You 36
37. The Path is More than Doing, It is in Being. 37
38. Don't Be Phony or Selfish on the Path. 38
39. The Peace and Spirit of the Path Fills Voids 39
40. Come Home and Be One with the Path. 40
41. The Path is Not Easy and Requires Sacrifice to Master . 41
42. Ying and Yang Work to Balance the Path 42
43. Gentleness Overcomes Strife 43
44. Do Not Desire Useless Material Possessions 44
45. The True Path is the Narrow Path 45
46. The True Path Brings Peace 46
47. No Special Education is Needed to Follow the Path . . . 47
48. Search for New Knowledge to Reach Full Potential . . . 48
49. Have Compassion and Forgiveness, not Grudges 49
50. Seeking Pleasures Does Not Satisfy 50
51. The Path Gives Meaning to Life. 51
52. Stay Close to the Path Until You Die 52

53. Don't Waste Time with Foolish Pleasures 53
54. Share the Path with Family, Country, and World. . . . 54
55. The True Path Brings Life, the Non-Path Brings Death . . . 55
56. You Are Responsible For Every Idle Word You Speak . . 56
57. Fairness and Respect Wins the People's Trust 57
58. Stay Away From Constant Fault-Finding 58
59. Use Good Judgment to Help the People. 59
60. The Path Guides Wise Rulers 60
61. Be Servants to Each Other and Prosper 61
62. Both Words and Deeds Help Your Journey 62
63. Make Honest Evaluations of Every Situation 63
64. Begin Projects Early. 64
65. Speak Honesty, Live With Integrity. 65
66. Humble, Giving Leaders Attract Support 66
67. Live With Love and Compassion 67
68. The Best Defense Is When Weapons Are Not Needed. . 68
69. Be Smart in Conflict and Keep Weapons Hidden 69
70. Wisdom Helps To Turn People from Selfish Desires. . . 70
71. Admit Your Wrongs and Don't Be a Know-it-All 71
72. Don't Control Others 72

73. Be Brave, but Take No Silly Risks 73
74. Don't Make Idle Threats or Instill Fear 74
75. Beware of Greedy Rulers Who Demand High Taxes. . . .75
76. Live Your Life like a Child. 76
77. Those Who Can Give Should Do So 77
78. Be Like Water and Be Persistent. 78
79. Keeping Your Promises Means Integrity. 79
80. Value and Enjoy the Simple Way of Life. 80
81. Focus On the Simplicity of Living the Wise Path 81
About The Author 83
Book Summary 85
About Ketna Publishing 87

INTRODUCTION

The Tao Te Ching is the most translated book in the world, next to the Bible. Unfortunately, even modern-day English translations are difficult to read at best, making this ancient wisdom of the Chinese unusable to modern Westerners and others who are hungry to apply its principles for a better life. Hence, the need for this book.

The Tao Te Ching, translated or known as the "Path of Virtue," was written about 600 BCE according to the Chinese by Laozi, also known as Lao Tzu or the "Old Master." However, the authenticity, dates, and authorship are still debated, as some claim even two authors were involved.

The Chinese have at least three translated versions of the Tao Te Ching, including some manuscripts dating back to 270 CE found by explorer Marc Aurel Stein in the Mogao Caves in the 1920s and 1930s.

In 1993, the oldest text version was found in a tomb near Guodian, written on bamboo tablets and dated before 300 BCE. This text was an exciting find, revealing fourteen unknown verses or "chapters."

Regardless, the eighty-one chapters or sections of the Tao Ching, composed of over 5,000 Chinese characters, make up a solid foundation for Taoism, Chinese philosophy, and Chinese Religion. They are also used as a primary source of creativity and inspiration by the Chinese and others worldwide.

The Tao Te Ching originated in two parts: the Tao Te Ching, which covers chapters 1-37, and the Te Ching, which covers chapters 38-81. Still, the complexity of the Chinese characters translated to various English versions left more riddles than answers. It made it a "tough reading" for those looking for a "quick" application of the wisdom within. Most English translations are mystical and obscure at best.

From these "summarized" verses, one will notice a correlation between Christian text and perhaps a "proverb" type reading. Christian missionaries connected Taoism, Christianity, the Tao Te Ching, and the New Testament.

These missionaries, and even some Chinese scholars, felt that Christian doctrine was mentioned, that Yahweh was inferred, and that a "great sage would come who would bring knowledge and peace to all men." Are world religions similar and not as different as they are supposed to be?

Indeed, when decoding the Tao Te Ching, I was amazed that its writing and meaning were not only deeply religious and spiritual, as we are accustomed to in Western society, but also very similar to the Bible in many verses and that both aspects of the Tao Te Ching and the Christian Bible are similar.

The eighty-one verses can take on a newer meaning and enlightenment for those who now read them. So that they will read smoothly in succession, I have omitted specific word-for-word translations and translated each verse as a whole instead to retain the flow, power, and understanding within.

I hope this modern, readable text that I present will open up discussions between people and help us understand each other in a world that tends to criticize differences or that which we do not understand.

So enjoy this book, apply its wisdom, and live in peace and love.

1
Follow the Right Path

The Path is not the heavenly Path per se, but rather the earthly Path and the way leading to Heaven. The Tao is more earthly advice to reach your goal. A higher power is the beginning of Heaven and Earth; thus, the question is asked: what is our plan on earth related to an unseen God and his higher power? Be certain you follow the right Path, or you will suffer evil consequences. The question is, will you follow good or evil? The question then becomes, what is good, and what is evil? What does God, your higher power want?

2

Live Without Judgment and Desire

Be careful not to judge a book by its cover; all things are not as they appear to be. There must be a blending of hardness and softness for the Path to work; there must be balance. There can be no desire (wu-wei); it just is. We can't change it, but we can only do our best with humility to follow the Path.

3
Be Humble and Treat People Well

Yes, be humble, don't praise some, and put people on a pedestal, which only brings jealousy from others. Don't brag about what you have and others don't. They will want or crave what you have as a result. There is no need to show off. To lead people, you must get them to trust you. Get them to relax, feed them, let them measure up, and strengthen them; then, you will not have to fear people scheming against you.

4

The Path Brings Love and Compassion

The Path is a wealth of Knowledge and encompasses many things. It brings love, compassion, and togetherness and is overflowing in this very thing.

5

You Must Live and Experience the Truth Path

God, your higher power, does not regard people lightly or with disregard. Heaven and earth are one, and they blend together along the journey, a journey that is not just talked about, but must be experienced.

6
Mother Earth Flows

The valley spirit or Mother Earth flows without effort, and its beginning is the 'root' of Mother Earth as we know it.

7
The Path Never Ends

Heaven, Earth, and God last forever, are never-ending, and live forever.

8

Gently Present the Path to Others

The Path must be absorbed, but it is difficult as men hate good and love evil thoughts and desired things. So, while on earth, think about what is good, approach these evil-doers with gentleness and self-control, and if you present the Path correctly without coercion, you won't be responsible for their fate.

9

Don't Brag, Boast, or Demand Your Way

Don't be one who always wants their way, caught up with greed and material things, puffed up with bragging and boasting, and eventually losing what you have.

10

Let Go of Material Possessions and Give

So let go of material goods and focus on the oneness of the Path, like a child just happy "to be." Live with balance in love and law when looking at others' points of view. Be able to give without expecting something back. Do your best and share wisdom, but don't be a know-it-all.

11

Don't Clutter Your Brain with Useless Things

This life path is a space to fill when you keep an open mind and are careful about your thoughts. Don't clutter your brain with useless things; keep an open mind to be receptive to the Path and what it offers.

12

Avoid Distractions and Seek the Eternal

To see too much, to hear too much, to experience too much, and gathering too much takes you off the Path. The King and goal of your life should be Heaven. Heaven is the Path to be sought after, and the Path is eternal. Even though the physical body dies, the spirit lives forever.

13

Be a Humble Servant

Be humble and without desire so you can stay on the Path. This attitude will keep you grounded and free from being ambushed with criticism, which often comes whether you gain much acclaim and fortune or when you lose it all. Yes, be at peace with yourself and be a servant, for if you help the world with your service, the world shall respond in kind.

14

The Spirit is the Beginning of the Path

The Path cannot be seen, cannot be heard, and cannot be touched, but when looking for it, listening for it, or reaching for it, it fills the senses, and those three things become one. It is shapeless and colorless and will exist from beginning to end. The Path has not changed from the start. The spirit is the beginning of the Path.

15

Make the Teachings of the Path Clear to All

Those who mastered the Path in the past did so wisely and experienced the spirit and Path profoundly. They mastered traits to make the journey successful, moving carefully and with caution, not getting sidetracked while also being wary of those things that could take them off course. Yet, they were open to others, continually took unclear teaching, and made it clear to all without the desire for personal gain. Learn from these past teachers.

16

Plant a Seed in Others

There is value in just "being". Do much with the little you have and do much for others; if you plant a seed in others, it will grow and be rewarded. There are times to be quiet in thought, reflection, sharing, and active in the journey. The Path is impartial, so acting on one's wishes instead of the Path does harm. So be receptive to the Path, for it leads to the Kingdom of Heaven, which is the way, and the way is eternal and lasts forever.

17

Make Your Path a Team Effort

The Path has been known, loved, and praised since the olden days, while some hated it. So be sincere and careful with your words, and work well with others so they feel it was a team effort, not you taking the credit for reaching specific goals. That way, all can share happily in the reward.

18

Be Wary of False Teachings

Be careful; when there are attempts to destroy the Path by the foolish intellect of some who claim they know the way, there is a loss of compassion, and then chaos and false teachers come forth.

19

Avoid False Devotion to God

Avoid false piety and morality while claiming "higher" wisdom. Where there is false giving to impress, those who horde riches will succumb to robbery. To sum this up, see the Path in its most accurate form so you will not be greedy with desire.

20

Following the Path Requires Sacrifice

The Path is a way that must be experienced and applied, and not just learned. Do not spend time dwelling on unanswered questions. The journey requires sacrifice; consider this: I am everywhere without a home, while others live happily with false joy. I may feel alone and tired, while others enjoy treasures here, but I leave material possessions behind to follow the Path. While these people seem happy and noticed, I am ignored and forgotten. I seem to have no place to rest, and everyone has goals. I may not understand this totally and know I am different, but I also see the root of the Path for my benefit carries me.

21

The Path is Driven by Faith and Belief

Remember that you can follow the good and right Path, but it cannot be defined. It's indescribable, with vast Knowledge driven by faith and belief. From the beginning of time to now, it has been around forever.

22

The Path Has All the Answers

The Path has all the answers for those who seek and are simplistic in their approach. One comes to recognize this and becomes an example for all. The Path is already complete and perfect; it does not need to force its way, brag, or desire, and it is not contentious. Believe in its completeness and follow it.

23

Only One Path is Complete

Don't try to change the world and create continuity; even Heaven and Earth cannot control certain events like the weather. Instead, focus on the Path; you and the Path will become one. Just like someone would become the same if the Path is wrong, either Path may appear to be a happy way to go, but only one Path is correct because people will only trust those on the right Path.

24

Don't Stray from the True Path

Stay balanced and don't stray from the Path, keep a low profile, don't confront people or brag, and stay humble. It is useless to go another way; if you do, it only feeds the ego and is disliked by all. Those who follow the Path do not do this.

25

Four Things Are Great

The Path was born before Heaven and Earth and continues as the "great path." This Path is greatness that transcends both time and place. Four things are great: the Path, Heaven, earth, and people. Because humans depend on the earth, the earth depends on Heaven, and Heaven depends on the Path.

26

Bear Your Heavy Burdens

Bare your heavy burdens, for the Path is not easy. Don't be distracted by things of this world; instead, focus on what needs to be done. Otherwise, you will lose the very foundation you and your family have and the ability to lead or show others the Path.

27

Teach the Path without Criticism

Don't create stress with fault finding, and then people will accept you, and in so doing, you can elevate them by lighting their Path. Those on the right Path must teach those who are not. You must first value and love these people to accomplish this goal.

28

Be an Example for Others

Be strong, gentle, open with people, and nonjudgmental. Be balanced, be an example, and stay on the Path, and your Path will be abundant. Listen and be one with the Path, and your Path will become whole.

29

Don't Try to Rule the World

Don't look to rule the world; otherwise, you will fail because of your greedy manipulation. Remember, sometimes things go right and sometimes wrong, and that's just how it is. Therefore, stay away from excess, overestimating your ability, trying to be great, and thus becoming overbearing.

30

Avoid War and the Wrong Path

Using the Path always ensures fairness and give-and-take. Otherwise, if you go to war with people, you dig your own grave. Learn quickly and stop this action. Yes, achieving is good, but don't brag about it. Achieve in humility without forcing your way onto others and bragging about this; this would be the non-path.

31

Avoid Using Weapons Whenever Possible

Using weapons is an unfavorable thing to do. No one likes them, and the man on the wise Path does not use them. Make your position one of peace and not war if you can. If not, have no joy in their use. Only those who like to kill are happy to use weapons, but no one will trust this person because regular citizens have to bury their own and will have to shed their tears, furthering distrust of those who use weapons.

32

You Don't Need a Fancy Title to Follow the Path

Don't worry about having a title; the Path does not need a big name or title to follow it. Have no fear, don't be misled, and remember many things will fall into place. Heaven and earth will have balance, and the heavens will open up. Some will be unable to cope and adjust to follow the Path, causing divisions among you. Knowing to stay on the Path will help you avoid falling.

33

True Power is Understanding Yourself and Others

If you understand others, you are intelligent. If you understand yourself, you are wise. Overcoming both yourself and others is power. Not being envious of others is to be rich. You live forever if you live with energy and passion and hold nothing back from following the Path.

34

The Path Reveals its Greatness if You Stay on It

The Path itself (or spirit) cannot be stopped. It requires much to survive, and though you can be slowed down or sidetracked temporarily, return to it without coercion, and it will show you why it is great.

35

The Path Will Bring You Rest and Peace

Hold to the Path, and you will rest in peace. Those who follow wine, food, and pleasure are distracted. The right Path is what you feel, the spirit, the way, and it's there for the taking.

36

Empty the Old You and Begin the New You

You must weaken your resistance, break down and forget the past, "empty out" the old, and then rebuild with the new. Illuminate that peace and gentleness overcome aggressiveness and fighting, the latter of which leads to failure.

37

The Path is More than Doing, It is in Being

The Path is not in doing but in being, yet encompasses all. Leaders should embrace it and keep an open mind rather than trying to force it unnaturally. If this happens, the heavens will be pleased.

38

Don't Be Phony or Selfish on the Path

Being moral on the surface is not real morality. Pretending to be friendly and putting on airs is false. True goodness and morality is not manipulative or done for selfish reasons. If you pretend to have a person's best interests at heart and don't, they will become angry with you. If you appear loyal and sincere and aren't, it will anger people. Deepness and thoroughness of being authentic and getting to know the whole situation instead of what a problem appears to look like is essential.

39

The Peace and Spirit of the Path Fills Voids

Wholeness is oneness. God's Path is clear: while life on earth is rough, the peace and spirit of the Path will fill the voids and lead to wholeness in life, especially when led by compassionate and effective rulers, as God does not want division. Without the Path, the earth would not be strong and peaceful, things would vanquish, and rulers would be ineffective. So, if you think of yourself as humble and follow the Path, greatness can develop because of the lack of desire for material things.

40

Come Home and Be One with the Path

Coming home and back to oneness with the Path will soften the Path's burden, help you honor your existence from your journey from a non-being to a being, and thus yield wisdom.

41

The Path is Not Easy and Requires Sacrifice to Master

Superior students hear the Path and follow it. Some in the middle listen to it, sometimes follow it, and sometimes fail to do so. A third group of people who don't understand it laugh it off. Perhaps this is because the Path is not easy and is long and tedious, which requires sacrifice and sometimes requires standing alone to reach the true self in a changing world as we explore the ends of the earth. It takes a long time to master the Path, and sometimes the good news it represents is hard to grasp and mysterious to some.

42

Ying and Yang Work to Balance the Path

Ying and Yang balance yield to each other for harmony in a deity-like way. Some may lose what they don't need, or it is not suitable for them. Some may gain something, whether a material possession or lose a desire that may hurt them. Impulsive force, demanding its way, leads to demise. Instead, yield to the Path.

43

Gentleness Overcomes Strife

Gentleness overcomes strife. The spirit moves, and you must react to the world in a positive way without personal gain; this is important.

44

Do Not Desire Useless Material Possessions

The useless or unnatural desire for material possessions and accumulation of things can come back to haunt you. Learning to balance and when to say "enough is enough" is an important lesson.

45

The True Path is the Narrow Path

Trying to be perfect without seeing the bigger picture of clarity and peace is useless. The Path may not seem grand to some and contradictory to others, and it requires walking a narrow path, but seeing the Path and becoming one with it is everything.

46

The True Path Brings Peace

There is peace when the Path is followed, and the country is not preparing for war. Realizing your current suffering is enough, be content with what you have, and remember that greed is bad.

47
No Special Education is Needed to Follow the Path

No special education is needed to know the Path and the way to Heaven. The more experience you have sometimes shows that less is known. Wise people learn this quickly.

48

Search for New Knowledge to Reach Full Potential

You must gather Knowledge. Following the Path, you let go of things you no longer need by gaining new Knowledge. These old things are left behind. Part of this self-actualization and reaching your full potential is peace. Let the world be; don't manipulate it for personal gain. For you, "Can gain the whole world and lose your soul."

49

Have Compassion and Forgiveness, not Grudges

Everyone is trying to do their best, so have no grudges but compassion and forgiveness for others. Don't expect too much, and you won't be disappointed. God, your higher power, loves unconditionally.

50

Seeking Pleasures Does Not Satisfy

Many people spend their lives actively seeking pleasures that do not fully satisfy them. Live life with passion but also with cautious intelligence.

51

The Path Gives Meaning to Life

The Path is the beginning that raises, guides, punishes, protects, and gives meaning and quality to life. The Path unfolds in a valuable way without coercion or force.

52

Stay Close to the Path Until You Die

The Path begins and out springs the fruit of this growth. Stay close to the Path until you die. Don't get involved in mundane things; focus on the Path, take time to notice the small things, yes, and be flexible so that you will be as "gentle as a dove and wary as a serpent."

53

Don't Waste Time with Foolish Pleasures

The Path involves sacrifice, so be wise and don't take shortcuts. For example, some spend time with "wine, women, and song" and only care about themselves. Be advised: This is not the Path to take.

54

Share the Path with Family, Country, and World

Take the wise and correct Path because it has been with us since the beginning and won't slip from your grip if you follow it. Previous generations have worshipped this same Path. So take the Path and spirit and pass it on to family, to the country, to the world.

55

The True Path Brings Life, the Non-Path Brings Death

Those who have morals, use fairness and have character are without attack. The grip of the Path gives lasting power and gives rise to harmony. It illuminates and nourishes life because of self-control and helps people grow; otherwise, they die. The Path blossoms and grows and leads to life. The non-path leads to death.

56

You Are Responsible For Every Idle Word You Speak

Everyone is responsible for every idle word they speak, so speak without anger and speak for peace or be silent. In this way, you benefit from "non-action." Even if you are right, you can cause strife even though those who speak do not know what they are saying. It's not worth it to prove them wrong. Let oneness be your goal, and the world will respond and notice.

57
Fairness and Respect Wins the People's Trust

Fairness wins people's trust, as does respecting those who oppose you. Accept the world without worry, and don't overregulate it. Too many laws, too many guns, more reliance on cleverness and deception, and poor interpretation of laws can lead to anger and rebellion. People will make good choices if they can live in peace and serenity without forcing their way.

58

Stay Away From Constant Fault-Finding

Relax and let people be; constant criticizing and micro-managing, constant fault finding, and even greed can ruin goodwill among you. The wise leader can get things done, correcting gently and without fault finding.

59

Use Good Judgment to Help the People

Use good judgment and be careful with your resources; you can overcome anything. Good decisions and sharing wisdom will bring confidence to people and allow you to be an effective, welcomed leader. This first begins with planting the roots of the Path in the people.

60

The Path Guides Wise Rulers

Wise Rulers govern with the Path of wisdom in mind; in doing so, there will be less evil as the people walk their Path and cause no harm.

61

Be Servants to Each Other and Prosper

Come together and be servants to each other, and there will be gain. People who want to work together will prosper. So, think of others before yourself.

62

Both Words and Deeds Help Your Journey

The Path of wisdom is already known by its worth. You can find peace here, as deeds and words will help your oneness with the Path. Great kings and riches cannot help you like the wisdom on the Path. The Path is without desire, so it has excellent worth.

63

Make Honest Evaluations of Every Situation

Get involved without acting; be sincere. Make an honest evaluation of the situation and respond to evil with good. In doing so, you can correct the situation early before the problem gets too big. Eliminating issues and problems while they are small means success. Do not delay; treat everything as a project of difficulty that needs to be dealt with quickly.

64

Begin Projects Early

Some things in life are apparent and well-explained. So it is with handling projects. Begin projects early before you dig a hole for yourself. Yes, start early and start immediately. Otherwise, you must rush to finish a project without planning, which usually fails. So be as careful and as thorough in the beginning as you are at the end, and you will have success. Therefore, a good leader not only plans but puts desires aside, learns people's hearts, and helps them without acting like their boss.

65

Speak Honesty, Live With Integrity

Speak with honesty and clarity. If you use deceit, you cheat the people, and these lies will catch up with you. People follow those with integrity, even though telling them what you think they want to hear sounds better.

66

Humble, Giving Leaders Attract Support

Consider the volume of the seas. The vastness of the sea equates to the volume of support from people. If you speak with humbleness and don't oppress them, not only will they accept you, but they will clamor for your leadership.

67

Live With Love and Compassion

The Path is great wisdom, so listen to it. Remember to live with compassion and love, within your means, with "no desire," and with consideration for others. Don't think of yourself as better than others. Have empathy for others and have something to give. Learn at your own pace, and do not rush to claim superiority or brilliance. Life is not worth living without giving others love and compassion. Rely on Heaven to accomplish these things, and your compassion will be rewarded with compassion.

68

The Best Defense Is When Weapons Are Not Needed

In methods of defense, be balanced, take no foolish risks, and keep your composure and wits about you. The best defense is one where attack or war is not needed. Treat these potential opponents as better than yourself and with respect as a "counterattack." There is a reward in appealing to a person's talent, defusing anger, and catching them doing something right. If you can do this, the heavens will rejoice.

69

Be Smart in Conflict and Keep Weapons Hidden

Know when to "hold them, and when to fold them." Know when to give ground in a debate or conflict. Keep your weapons hidden; use this "surprise" attack where you can accomplish much without a fight. Keep a proper respect for opponents and don't take anyone for granted; if you do so, it could mean defeat.

70

Wisdom Helps To Turn People from Selfish Desires

These laws of wisdom come from experience and the way of the Path. Yet many need to understand the Path or practice its teachings. If all people could understand me, I would not be required to help them. However, they don't, so I am valuable because people follow their worldly and selfish desires.

71
Admit Your Wrongs and Don't Be a Know-it-All

Again, don't be a know-it-all. Admit your wrongs and that you don't know everything, and you will earn respect. Not knowing and thinking you do is both arrogance and illness.

72

Don't Control Others

Lead without coercion, and you will win the people over. Please don't get into their business and use it against them to keep them down. This understanding helps you to respect yourself and others if you let go of the desire to control others.

73

Be Brave, but Take No Silly Risks

If you choose between being brave and foolish and being brave, pick being brave without taking silly risks. Even leaders can't understand Heaven and its ways, even when Knowledge is given freely and without having to take foolish chances. So relax, don't worry, and set goals. Reach out and listen to others. Heaven has vast resources, but there is a right way to do it. So, combine your courage with intelligence.

74

Don't Make Idle Threats or Instill Fear

Don't make idle threats. If you constantly instill fear, you will make the people hate you, and they will revolt. Idle threats are not your job; leave this for someone else; otherwise, you harm yourself.

75

Beware of Greedy Rulers Who Demand High Taxes

People starve because of greedy rulers who demand high taxes. If you create contempt in others, they will not fear you. Therefore, think of others and not just yourself and be at peace.

76

Live Your Life like a Child

Live your life as a child would: be accepting, soft, open, and gentle instead of harsh, cold, bitter, and critical. Be flexible in your position instead of unwavering and cynical.

77

Those Who Can Give Should Do So

Those who can give should do so instead of the way some become increasingly greedy and steal from the poor or don't help at all. Yes, taking the Path on Earth leads to Heaven. So give with selflessness, full of generosity and kindness, and without bragging.

78

Be Like Water and Be Persistent

Take a clue from the water, which is persistent with success. Unlike the rock, which the flow of water can wear down, water is persistent yet gentle. If you accept corruption, it will become your master. So take this fact, stay on the Path, focus on the goal, and like water, you will be a success.

79

Keeping Your Promises Means Integrity

Again, let me remind you not to get angry and interfere in other people's business because people hold grudges and will not forget. Keeping your promises means integrity. Broken promises mean a lack of integrity.

80

Value and Enjoy the Simple Way of Life

Remember what is important. Value life and enjoy it. Protect yourself and stay out of quarrels. Remember the simple way of life, for this is precious. If you genuinely give people what they desire regarding food, clothes, and shelter, they will be at peace with their neighbors.

81

Focus On the Simplicity of Living the Wise Path

Be straightforward in speech, and don't argue. Instead, focus on the Path's simplicity instead of the examination's complexity. Therefore, learn the Path by experiencing it. For even these educated men are mere foolishness in their understanding, while those uneducated who follow the Path are the ones who understand all. Remember, we have a giving God, not a selfish God, who puts us on the right Path, for Heaven is here to help and not harm us. So follow the Path of wisdom set forth here.

ABOUT THE AUTHOR

Kevin M. Thomas is an award-winning author of titles like *Tao Te Ching Decoded*, *Living the Life of Proverbs*, *Commands of the New Testament*, *Why Daughters Need Their Dads*, *Wisdom and Virtue*, *The Great Path*, *Chinese Spiritual Thoughts*, and *The Happiest Women*. He has a varied background in Medicine, Alternative Health, Counseling, Religion, and Mind-Body Healing and is an Ordained Deacon Minister.

Kevin is passionate about promoting and delivering positive change to anyone. He strives to effect personal growth in individuals via Mind-Body-Spirit research and application. Finally, he considers his spiritual relationship with God and unconditional love for his children, Isiah, Caroline, Kimberly, Cheyenne, and the rest of his supportive family, including Erik, his most fabulous treasures.

BOOK SUMMARY

Tao Te Ching De-Coded is an easy-to-understand Paraphrased Summary of the true life force and the Path for right living that has been passed down for centuries. This version of the second most translated in the world helps you *actually* understand what it takes to live a simpler, happier, and more disciplined life with less stress. It comes from the foundation of Taoism and Chinese Philosophy and Religion and focuses on true wisdom.

ABOUT KETNA PUBLISHING

Kevin Thomas and Erik Naugle own KETNA Publishing, a small hometown publisher in mid-Michigan. Their goal is to deliver high-quality information to people so they can positively change their lives by applying body, mind, and spirit principles.

You can contact KETNA Publishing at grobthom@aol.com or write to KETNA Publishing, P.O. Box 90861, Burton, Michigan, 48509.

www.ingramcontent.com/pod-product-compliance
Lightning Source LLC
Chambersburg PA
CBHW070119080526
44586CB00013B/1339